# 101 Lesser Known Facts Related to the Attack on Pearl Harbor

## Douglas T. Shinsato

Cover Print, Black Ships and Samurai in Edo Bay, by Toshu Shogetsu
Permission of the University of Tokyo, The Historiographical Institute

First Paperback Edition 2013

ISBN: 0984674543
ISBN-13: 9780984674541
Library of Congress Control Number: 2013940233
eXperience, inc.
Kamuela, HI

# Table of Contents

# Foreword

by
Shigehiko Togo

I have known Douglas Shinsato for many years, and I am pleased that he has put together "101 Facts" that help to explain the events leading up to the Pacific War.

Any major war—especially one as enormous and catastrophic as the Pacific War—does not have a single cause. Even identifying several causes requires over-simplification.

In my view, those several causes were:

The political, economic and military tensions that resulted in World War II were fundamentally based on the huge divide between Fascist and Democratic countries;

The economic conflict over the Asia market is often over-looked by historians. All the major Western powers had colonial footholds in Asia and sought to reap the benefits from Asia's energy and agricultural resources and her population;

The political conflict for hegemony over their Asian colonies was a key factor in policy-making for the Western powers. After the end of World War II, Great Britain, France and the Netherlands used military force to attempt to maintain their control over Malaya (now Malaysia), French Indochina (now Vietnam) and the Dutch East Indies (now Indonesia);

Japan and the United States both had colonies in Asia, which made them "equals" and put them in a situation which increased the probability of a military conflict; and

Japan's accession to the Tripartite Agreement increased tensions with America and added the Soviet Union—which was a non-democratic, fascist country—as a potential anti-Tripartite combatant.

The "101 Facts" you are about to read cover what I believe are the major reasons that Japan went to war with the Allies, in general, and the United States, specifically. They cover the political, military, economic and diplomatic issues surrounding the decision to attack Pearl Harbor.

I have written many articles and a book about the diplomatic history related to the Pacific War. My grandfather, Shigenori Togo, was Japan's Foreign Minister from October, 1941 until September, 1942. He tried to prevent war with the United States and was removed from the Cabinet. When it was clear that Japan would go down in defeat, in April, 1945, Prime Minister Kantaro Suzuki asked him to join the Cabinet in an effort to end the war.

I know that you will enjoy this concise book of facts leading up to the attack on Pearl Harbor.

# Foreword

by
Elaine B. Fischel

Pearl Harbor...how did this lovely lagoon nestled in the hills of Oahu go from being a place—a name—to a "date that will live in infamy"?

We knew Hawaii as "the loveliest fleet of islands anchored in any ocean." So said Mark Twain in the 1800s. Little did he dream that within one hundred years, those beloved islands would be stripped of their beauty by the horrors of war.

You are about to discover how that happened; how those little "yellow" men from the tiny country of Japan attacked Pearl Harbor and crippled the mighty fleet of the United States. What were those people like? Did they dream of conquering America or rather hitting her so hard she would have trouble rising to her feet to fight the battles she was destined to fight?

We know Pearl Harbor as the place where America was attacked. But Pearl Harbor's place in history is so much more than the images the "sneak attack" created. Was it a "sneak attack?" Our history does not tell us of the plans made by the United States decades before Pearl Harbor as to how this country would be defended were it attacked.

What do we know of Japan—a country isolated from the rest of the world up until the 1860s when the Meiji Revolution brought her onto the international scene? How did it happen that Japan modeled her Navy on the Royal Navy of Great Britain; her Army on that of Germany?

This book is a treasure of information brought to life by the meticulous research of the author. We owe Douglas Shinsato many debts of gratitude for revealing to us how a nation can rise, be destroyed and rise again. This is a book of facts, of history, of military and social psychology. But most important it is about PEOPLE who made it happen. You are about to embark upon a voyage you will long remember and cherish.

# Author's Note

This book is a compilation of lesser-known facts surrounding events leading up to and following the attack on Pearl Harbor in December, 1941.

Most of the information here is the by-product of research I did for my translation work on two manuscripts: The first, into English, was the autobiography of Mitsuo Fuchida, leader of the attack on Pearl Harbor; the second, into Japanese, the memoirs of Elaine Fischel, a member of the American legal team at the Tokyo War Crimes Trial that defended Japan's top three admirals and the Emperor's political advisor.

This compilation of lesser-known facts is intended as a short "tourist's guide" to the attack on Pearl Harbor. It covers events and participants from as far back as 1853 with the arrival of the U.S. Navy's Black Ships in Tokyo Bay and ends with present day assessments of the attack that is regarded as a turning point in world history. Some facts need only a few words, others several paragraphs.

A number of the facts are related to laws, legislative bills and court rulings. This is partly because of my legal training many decades ago but mostly because I believe that the legal atmospherics—while certainly not perfect evidence—are a good indicator of the mind-set of the community leaders of a society or of what government leaders can impose on their constituents without too much resistance.

I am most grateful to my friends for their contributions to this book:

- Shigehiko Togo, journalist and author of the biography of his grandfather, Shigenori Togo, Japan's wartime Foreign Minister; and

- Elaine Fischel, author of *Defending the Enemy*, and currently still a practicing lawyer.

For their comments and responses to my many questions, I would also like to thank:

- Ed Miller, author of *War Plan Orange* and *Bankrupting the Enemy*;

- Vice Admiral (Retired) Yoji Koda, Fleet Commander of the Japanese Self-Defense Maritime Forces;

- Carol Petillo, author of *Douglas MacArthur: The Philippine Years*; and

- Marie and Joe Yoshiya Fuchida, daughter-in-law and son of Captain Mitsuo Fuchida.

Thanks also to my editor and dearest partner, my wife Jennifer, for her invaluable contributions.

August 2013

Douglas Shinsato
Waikii Ranch
Hawaii

# 101 Lesser Known Facts Related to the Attack on Pearl Harbor

**Fact #1: 1853—U.S. Navy Gunboats in Tokyo Bay**

In July 1853, U.S. Navy Commodore Matthew Perry sailed into Tokyo Bay with his four Black Ships and demanded that Japan open trade relations with the United States. In the mid-19th Century, proper society's term for this kind of international negotiating strategy was Gunboat Diplomacy. Japan had enforced a policy of isolation for over two centuries, but it was clear to the Shogunate leaders that they did not have the military capability to repulse the U.S. fleet. The forcible opening of Japan set in motion a civil war that pitted the Shogun Loyalists against the Reformers. The centuries-old Tokugawa Shogunate collapsed, and the Imperial system was reinstituted in 1867, which we know as the Meiji Restoration.

**Fact #2: Jardine Matheson—British Trading Firm**

Jardine Matheson was founded in China in 1832 by Scotsmen William Jardine and James Matheson. It began by shipping primarily opium and silk and grew to become one of the world's largest trading firms.

Jardine Matheson was the first foreign company in Japan, registered one year after the opening of the Port of Yokohama in 1858.

In 1859, Thomas Glover, a Scot, joined Jardine Matheson in Japan. Subsequently, he founded Glover Trading Company and, using Jardine Matheson ships, helped to purchase the gunpowder and rifles for the rebel leaders who would overthrow the Shogunate. Glover worked closely with Takayoshi Kido, who kept an extensive diary of the events surrounding the civil war. Kido studied modern artillery applications and deployment and supervised the construction of one of Japan's first Western-style warships. He was one of the main actors in the formation of the new revolutionary government. Two generations later, his grandson, Koichi Kido, became Emperor Hirohito's closest political advisor and was the author of a diary that was used extensively by lawyers at the Tokyo War Crimes Trial.

## Fact #3: The Boshin War

The movie, *The Last Samurai*, was based largely on events following the Boshin War between the ruling Tokugawa Shogunate and the pro-Imperial western clans (Satsuma, Choshu and Tosa). One of Japan's best known *samurai*, Saigo Takamori, played a key role in the overthrow of the Shogunate but later led a rebellion against the Imperial Army.

In response to the forced opening of Japan by the U.S. Navy, the pro-Imperial rebels had been reorganizing their military for nearly a decade—focusing on acquiring modern weaponry and training. In the final months of the Boshin Civil War, they besieged the castle town of Aizu, one of the last outposts of Shogunate Loyalists. The defenders fought a swords-vs.-guns battle they could not win, and in November, 1868, the leaders of the pro-Shogunate Aizu clan surrendered. The consequences were tragic for the Loyalists. The White Tigers (*Byakkotai*), a group of 16- and 17-year-old *samurai* from prominent families, committed suicide en masse, and the wives of many prominent Loyalists took their children's lives before killing themselves to avoid the dishonor of capture.

Following the restoration of the Imperial system, Saigo Takamori came to disagree with the central government's policies of modernization. In 1877, he led the Satsuma Rebellion. At the Battle of Shiroyama, the final encounter of the rebellion, his troops ran out of ammunition, and they fought with swords, bows and arrows. Saigo Takamori died in this battle.

## Fact #4: Tokyo is Born

On October 26, 1868, the city of Edo was renamed Tokyo, which means Eastern Capital. Although the population had declined significantly due to the civil war, it was still a large metropolis. In fact, in the 1790s, Edo had over 1.2 million people—double the number in London—making it the world's most populous city.

## Fact #5: The Establishment of the Imperial Japanese Navy

In light of their experience with the U.S. Navy's black ships, Japan's new leaders were quick to understand the importance of naval power. In July 1868, the government established the Imperial Japanese Navy (IJN)—or *Dai-Nippon Teikoku Kaigun*. After intensive study by various study missions, an Imperial Decree was issued in 1870 declaring that the IJN would be modeled after the British Royal Navy, then the world's largest and most powerful fleet.

## Fact #6: The Meiji Constitution and Human Rights

At the same time as it was modernizing its military, the Japanese government sent many of its premier scholars to the West to study the legal systems and the constitutions of the world's leading economic powers. In 1890, the government enacted the Meiji Constitution, based largely on the Prusso-German constitutional monarchy.

Significantly, on the subject of human rights, the new constitution recognized freedom of expression as guaranteed only "within limits of the law;" these, in turn, were not defined. Subsequently, such laws were further interpreted or amended to maximize government control over free speech.

Controls like these provided the basis for the passage of a series of Public Security Preservation Laws, beginning in 1894, which, in turn, provided the framework for the 1925 establishment of the Thought Police, or *Tokko*.

## Fact #7: Japan's Public Security Preservation Law of 1925

Under this law, individuals with opinions opposed to the government could be sentenced to jail terms. The definition of what constituted opposition was so vague that anyone branded as an opponent of the government could be imprisoned.

In the same year, in order to implement and enforce this law, the government created the Thought Police within the Home Ministry. The Thought Police played an important role prior to and during the Pacific War and were known for their surveillance of Socialists, Communists and, later, anti-militarists.

## Fact #8: Amendments to the Public Security Preservation Law of 1925

The basic law was amended in 1928 and again in 1941. It allowed for preventative detention of political activists who opposed the government. It also legalized the indefinite detention of political prisoners and did not require the government to formally charge detainees with a specific crime.

## Fact #9: Impact of the Public Security Preservation Law

As a result of the government's broad arrest-and-imprisonment powers, the 1930s in Japan were a decade of *"gekokujou,"* or the concept of overthrow from below. Prevalent during the Warring States Period (1467-1573), *gekokujou* resulted in the overthrow of feudal lords by their retainers. During the 1930s, justifying their "moral actions" based on this concept, junior Imperial Japanese Army (IJA) officers moved against their superiors, who were viewed as too moderate, and frequently assassinated politicians who were viewed as opponents of militarism and empire-building. Under the Public Security Preservation Law, insubordination—and even assassination attempts—received light sentences.

Extremists in the military increasingly rose against moderates in the government. Each incident increased the influence and, eventually, the dominance of the IJA within the Japanese government.

## Fact #10: The IJN Grows in Tandem with Japan's Quest for Empire

Initially organized for coastal defense, the IJN gradually increased the size of its fleet. Its orientation towards defensive-only capabilities changed in the mid-1870s as the IJN gained fighting experience with incursions against Taiwan and Korea.

In the 1894-95 Sino-Japanese War, the IJN defeated the Chinese Navy and learned several key lessons: primarily that the IJN would require more capital ships—battleships and destroyers—in order to defeat enemy navies which were supplied by German shipyards.

Following the Sino-Japanese War, the world's leading colonial powers took advantage of China's weakened situation and increased their control over Chinese territory and trade. In 1900, an anti-foreign and anti-Christian Chinese nationalist movement instigated what became known as the Boxer Rebellion. The so-called Eight-Nation Alliance—Austria-Hungary, the United States, Italy, France, Germany, Japan, Russia, and the United Kingdom—sent in 20,000 troops and a naval task force to quash this insurrection. The IJN deployed with the navies of the West and provided 18 of the 50 ships that eventually suppressed the rebellion.

In addition to providing battle experience and confidence boosters to the relatively young IJN, these naval victories set the stage for Japan's next significant military initiative.

### Fact #11: The Emergence of Japan as a Pacific Power

In 1904, Czarist Russia and Japan went to war. The following year, at the Battle of Tsushima, Admiral Heihachiro Togo effectively annihilated the Russian Asiatic and Baltic Fleets. The IJN sank 21 of 38 Russian ships, captured seven and disarmed six—killing 4,545 Russian servicemen and taking 6,106 prisoners. The IJN lost only 116 men and three torpedo boats.

This defeat for Russia was followed by mutinies in the Russian Navy and contributed to the start of the Russian Revolution in 1905.

### Fact #12: Early U.S. Concerns about Japan

As a result of its victory in the Spanish-American War, the U.S. acquired the Philippines as a colony in 1898. At the same time, Japan was emerging as the other major military force in Asia owing to its successes against China in 1900 and its destruction of the

Russian Asiatic and Baltic Fleets in 1905. Moreover, the increasing focus of Western powers was away from Asia and toward the increasing political tensions in Europe.

In response to Japan's emergence as a regional power, the U.S. Navy began war planning exercises against the IJN in 1905. The tactical and strategic operational plans, known as War Plan Orange, went through many modifications over the next 35 years.

The decades between 1905 and the attack on Pearl Harbor saw an on-going battle between the "Thrusters," who favored a rush to the Western Pacific for a quick victory over the IJN, and the "Cautionaries," who favored a step-by-step, island-hopping war of attrition over the smaller nation.

After the attack on Pearl Harbor, the Cautionaries' strategies that were developed during the initial years of War Plan Orange were implemented by Fleet Admirals William Leahy (Chief of Staff to the Commander in Chief, President Franklin Roosevelt) and Chester Nimitz (Commander in Chief, Pacific Fleet) because, first, the Allied leaders had decided on a strategy of Germany First, and, second, the U.S. Navy did not have the capacity to wage a full two-ocean war in the early years of WWII.

**Fact #13: Ascendency of the Imperial Japanese Army (IJA)**

In 1906, the Kwantung Garrison, a unit of the Imperial Japanese Army (IJA) was deployed to protect Japan's commercial interests on the Liaolong Peninsula, Manchuria. These territories had come under Japanese control as a result of the Russo-Japan War.

Following World War I, the population of Japan grew very rapidly, outstripping the country's ability to provide enough food or jobs. Attention began to turn to Manchuria as a potential source of rice and food crops for Japan's growing and hungry population.

By 1920, the Kwantung Garrison had been reorganized into the Kwantung Army, an elite imperialist unit whose leaders believed in pushing all European colonial rulers out of Asia and enlarging the Japanese Empire. In 1931, the Kwantung Army engineered a "terrorist" incident that led to the invasion of Manchuria. In 1932, Japan formally established the region as a colony, renaming it Manchukuo. This set the stage for the start of the Sino-Japan War in 1937.

## Fact #14: Japanese Immigration to the United States

Beginning in 1900, tens of thousands of Japanese migrated to the U.S. because of the lack of jobs and a scarcity of food in Japan. According to U.S. government population data, the number of registered Japanese nationals grew each decade before slowing as a result of the 1924 U.S. Immigration Act.

## Fact #15: 1907 Gentlemen's Agreement between the U.S. and Japan

By 1905, the influx of Japanese immigrants into California had created an anti-Japanese backlash. In Northern California, local citizens formed a Japanese and Korean Exclusion League, and one of their demands was the segregation of Japanese from white school children.

In 1906, the San Francisco Board of Education instituted a ruling that required all students of Japanese ancestry to attend separate non-white schools. The Japanese government protested, and, in order to reduce tensions between the two Pacific naval powers, President Theodore Roosevelt crafted a compromise.

Under the Gentlemen's Agreement—an Executive Order signed by Roosevelt—Japan agreed to end the issuance of passports to Japanese laborers, and the San Francisco Board of Education agreed to allow children of Japanese descent to attend public schools.

The restrictions on immigration did not apply to Hawaii, then a U.S. Territory, where American plantation owners depended on laborers from Japan and the rest of Asia. Japanese nationals who emigrated to Hawaii were not restricted from moving to the mainland U.S under the Gentlemen's Agreement.

**Fact #16: 1913 California Alien Land Law Ban**

Racial tensions continued to grow. In 1913, California passed the Alien Land Law, which barred aliens who were deemed not eligible for citizenship from purchasing or entering long-term leases of land.

This law was aimed primarily at the Japanese population and amended by a 1920 state ballot initiative. The Alien Land Laws, as they were referred to, were upheld by the U.S. Supreme Court in 1923 on the grounds that they were not in violation of the Equal Protection Clause of the 14th Amendment. (It was not until 1952 that the California Supreme Court invalidated these laws as unconstitutional.)

**Fact #17: U.S. Immigration Act of 1924**

The Federal Immigration Act of 1924, signed into law by President Calvin Coolidge in May of that year, included both the National Origins and the Asian Exclusion Acts. This national law set limits on the number of people who could immigrate into the U.S. based on country of origin. The provisions of the Asian Exclusion Act banned all immigration from Asian countries—including Japan.

According to a recent study on the history of U.S. immigration, this new law was so restrictive that in 1924 more immigrants from Japan left the U.S. than arrived.

## Fact #18: Redistribution of Colonial Territories after World War I

The defeat of Germany and the Ottoman Empire in 1918 resulted in the wholesale re-distribution of colonial territories, the re-drawing of national borders and the creation of new nation-states across Europe, North Africa and the Middle East.

The League of Nations awarded Japan, for fighting on the winning side, control over the German concessions in China and the South Pacific Mandate, which included Palau, the Northern Mariana Islands, the Federated States of Micronesia, and the Marshall Islands. Many of these islands had natural harbors and inlets ideal for use as naval anchorages, a fact which increased the level of concern among planners in the U.S. Navy.

As events unfolded, many of these islands saw major Pacific War battles between the U.S. and Japan.

## Fact #19: Japan's World War I Naval Engagement in Europe

Because of its limited engagement in World War I European naval battles, the IJN did not have extensive first-hand experience of the devastating effectiveness of Germany's torpedo-carrying U-boats. This was to have a major impact on Japan's design and production strategies of its submarines prior to and during the Pacific War.

**Fact #20: The Rise of Air Power and Captain Osami Nagano**

Osami Nagano graduated from the Japanese Naval Academy in 1900 and studied at Harvard Law School from 1913-15. He lived in the Brookline, Massachusetts home of Mr. and Mrs. C. E. Wheeler, whom he called his "American father and mother."

In 1921, Captain Osami Nagano was the Naval Attaché at the Japanese Embassy in Washington, D.C. In July of that year, he witnessed General Billy Mitchell's "Aircraft vs. Battleship" Naval Bombing Experiments at Virginia Capes, the entrance to Chesapeake Bay.

Mitchell was a strong advocate of air power and used the "Aircraft vs. Battleship" exercise to demonstrate the superiority of the new aviation technology. After accusing U.S. Army and Navy leaders of an "almost treasonable administration of the national defense" for investing in battleships instead of aircraft carriers and fighter planes, Mitchell was court-martialed for insubordination.

The court, which included Major General Douglas MacArthur as a judge, found Mitchell guilty. He resigned from the Army but became a folk hero for his visionary ideas.

After he returned to Japan, Nagano was promoted to Rear Admiral and became an important proponent within the IJN of air power and the aircraft carrier.

**Fact #21: Washington Naval Conference of 1921-22**

As a result of the destruction and financial cost of World War I, the world's leading naval powers were eager to agree to capacity limitations. Although France and Italy attended this conference, the negotiations were dominated by the U.S., the United Kingdom, and Japan.

The five nations reached an agreement that set a limit on battleships, known as the 5:5:3 Ratio. In effect, this meant that for every five capital ships that the U.S. and the U.K. were allowed, Japan was allowed to have three.

The rationale for this limitation was the then conventional thinking that a fleet required a 70 percent capacity advantage over an enemy fleet in order to win a sea battle. Furthermore, the accepted thinking was that a fleet loses 10 percent of its fighting capacity for every 1000 nautical miles it sails. The U.S. Navy's expectation was that it would have to sail 3000 nautical miles to the Western Pacific and that the IJN would have to sail 1,500 nautical miles to engage the U.S. fleet. By the time they were in position to begin their battle, a 5-to-3 ratio would put the US and Japan almost at parity in terms of effective fighting capacity.

The intention was that neither side would have a perceived capacity advantage. However, the IJN saw this as an insult and a failure of the Western powers to recognize Japan as a political and military equal.

**Fact #22: London Naval Conferences of 1930 and 1934**

At the Washington Naval Conference, the U.S. and U.K. had a serious dispute over limitations on cruiser capacity. At the London Conference of 1930, agreements were reached on tonnage restrictions for heavy cruisers, light cruisers and auxiliary ships. At the Conference in 1934, the Japanese effectively withdrew from the treaty agreements and began a major shipbuilding program.

Rear Admiral Isoroku Yamamoto attended the 1930 Conference as a delegate. Later promoted to Vice Admiral, he attended the 1934 Conference as Japan's representative.

## Fact #23: The February 26, 1936 Incident

On February 26, 1936, young extremist IJA officers—strong believers in the Imperial Way, a doctrine which put domestic development ahead of expansion through war—staged a coup d'état. The goal of these officers was to eliminate their expansionist and pro-war rivals from the ranks of the government and military. The rebels assassinated several political leaders and succeeded in occupying the major government buildings of Tokyo. However, because of a case of mistaken identity, they failed to assassinate Prime Minister Keisuke Okada. They also failed in their attempt to take control of the Imperial Palace.

Major General Tomoyuki Yamashita, who was to play a key role throughout the Pacific War, was sympathetic to the rebels and attended several meetings with coup leaders. But his loyalty to the Emperor won out, and he reported the results of his meetings to the Imperial Palace.

IJA factions loyal to the Imperial Palace, which was angered by the attempted coup, moved quickly against the rebels. And the IJN, which historically did not involve itself in political matters, moved 40 ships to Tokyo Bay as a move to warn off IJA divisions that sided with the rebels. (One of many reasons for their deployment was that Prime Minister Okada was an IJN admiral.)

Tensions remained high until the rebels surrendered on February 29th. In closed trials, 19 of the rebel leaders were sentenced to death, and 40 were sent to prison. The military courts decided not to arrest other officers who were sympathetic to the rebel cause because doing so would have depleted the ranks of trained officers too severely.

This outcome meant that the radical Imperial Way faction lost its influence within the IJA. Furthermore, it brought to a close the period of "government by assassination," and the military—especially the pro-war faction of the IJA—increased its control over the civilian government.

## Fact #24: IJA in China

During the 1930s, China was dismembering into warring factions and was on the path to becoming a failed state. In July, 1937, following the exchange of gunfire between the Chinese and Japanese armies at the Marco Polo Bridge outside Beijing, the IJA deployed several hundred thousand troops to counter what they claimed was a Chinese attack. Within 17 months, with an expeditionary force that had expanded to 700,000 troops, Japan seized 700,000 square miles of Chinese territory and gained control over 170 million people.

Although this amounted to the Second Sino-Japan War, the government and press in Japan always referred to this war as "The China Incident." What followed was something the IJA did not anticipate or expect: By 1939, the Chinese Nationalists and the Communists agreed to a temporary cessation of their civil war hostilities in order to focus on defeating the Japanese.

## Fact #25: Draining the Japanese Treasury

By 1938, the IJA had committed 1,500,000 troops to China. W. P. Willmott, the noted British war historian, calculated that this represented one Japanese soldier for every 2.5 acres of conquered ground. Furthermore, the China Incident meant that 70 percent of Japan's budget was being earmarked for military expenditures.

## Fact #26: Japan's Reliance on Silk Exports

In *Bankrupting the Enemy*, an outstanding analysis of the economic and financial influences on the road to war, Edward

Miller points out how important silk was to Japan's economic well-being.

In the 1930s, raw silk accounted for two-thirds of all Japan's exports to America. Japanese raw silk was considered the finest in the world, and the basis for Japan's dominance in this category was two-fold: superior processes for harvesting threads from silkworm cocoons and comparatively low labor costs. This single commodity generated 57 percent of Japan's U.S. dollar revenues.

On the other side of the Pacific Ocean, the U.S. imported 100 percent of its raw silk from Japan, and 95 percent of this was used for the manufacture of women's expensive hosiery.

All of this changed on "Nylon Day"—May 15, 1939—at the New York Worlds Fair, when DuPont & Company introduced its new artificial silk, namely nylon, stocking. The stockings were a fashion hit, and Japan's silk sales plunged. This had an immediate and dramatic impact on Japan's ability to generate dollars, which were the lifeblood of its war material purchases.

## Fact #27: America in the 1930s—Oil Powerhouse of the World

In the 1930s, America was the world's largest oil producer. At the start of the next decade, the U.S. produced 63 percent of the world's output of crude oil. It imported only 9 percent of its energy needs. Japan, on the other hand, imported 80 percent of its oil from the U.S.

## Fact #28: Isolationism in the U.S.

During the 1930s, still recovering from the financial devastation of the Great Depression, America was a deeply divided country. Isolationists wanted nothing to do with the political and military turmoil in Europe or Asia. Internationalists believed that it was a national duty to intervene wherever America could make a difference.

The extent of the division is illustrated in the 1938 attempt by U.S. Representative Louis Ludlow, a Democrat, to introduce a bill requiring that a national referendum be held before a President could declare war. The House voted by 209-188 to refer Ludlow's bill back to the House Judiciary Committee, where it died.

**Fact #29: London Naval Conference and the U.S. Navy**

Because of the impact of the Great Depression, the U.S. government allocated limited funds for military expenditures. This meant that the U.S. Navy did not build up to treaty limitation maximums until 1937.

Without the continuing and special push by House Representative Carl Vinson, the IJN would have had superiority of numbers in every type of ship category over the U.S. Pacific Fleet through the 1940s.

**Fact #30: Don't Ask, Don't Tell**

Due to the bitter disputes between Isolationists and Internationalists, at Congressional appropriations hearings, politicians and U.S. Navy leaders talked only about defensive capabilities when they sought funding for new ship construction—even when proposed spending authorizations were for offensive weapons.

**Fact #31: June 1940—The Move to Pearl Harbor**

In June, 1940, President Franklin Roosevelt ordered the Pacific Fleet to be moved from San Diego to Pearl Harbor. The President wanted to show the Japanese that the U.S. had a powerful naval force that was capable of protecting its interests in the Philippines and of reaching Japan. This move also put the Pacific Fleet within striking distance of the IJN Carrier Task Force.

Vice Admiral (Retired) Yoji Koda, born in 1949, made an interesting observation about this move at the 70th Anniversary of the Commemoration of the Attack on Pearl Harbor. Before his retirement, he was the Fleet Commander of Japan's Maritime Self-Defense Force, a position that was at the same rank as Admiral Isoroku Yamamoto, Commander of the Combined Fleet. Koda graduated from Japan's National Defense Academy—successor to the disbanded Imperial Army Academy—and, during the course of his career, studied at Harvard University and was later a faculty member of the U.S. Naval War College. In Koda's opinion, the leaders of the IJN in 1940 considered Roosevelt's order to move the Pacific Fleet to Pearl Harbor to be an unofficial declaration of war.

## Fact #32: War Planners' Perception of the American Public's Tolerance for War

In 1940, judging that America would be pulled into the military turmoil in Europe and Asia, the Office of Naval Intelligence in Washington, D.C. concluded that the U.S. public would not tolerate a war that lasted into 1946. In *War Plan Orange*, Edward Miller writes that Admiral Charles "Savvy" Cooke, Chief War Plans Officer, predicted that Victory in Europe Day would take place in mid-1945.

In contrast, Admiral Isoroku Yamamoto, his future enemy on the other side of the Pacific Ocean, was ready to gamble that the U.S. military—not the public—would lose the will to continue fighting by 1943.

## Fact #33: U.S. Naval Expansion Acts of June and July 1940

Passed largely due to the efforts of Congressman Vinson, what became known as the Two-Ocean Navy Act authorized funding for the construction of:

• 17 battleships,
• 18 aircraft carriers,
• 29 cruisers,
• 115 destroyers and
• 42 submarines.

Many of these ships came into service in 1943 and under the command of Admiral Chester Nimitz, Commander in Chief of the Pacific Fleet.

## Fact #34: Yamamoto's Opinion on IJN War Planning

As late as August, 1939, Yamamoto was against initiating a war with America: "For the first six months of a conflict I will run like a wild boar, and for the first two years we will prevail; but after that, I am not at all sure of events."

In his letter of January 7, 1941 to Navy Minister Koshiro Oikawa, Yamamoto expressed his doubt about the IJN's ability to succeed with its strategy of *"yogei sakusen"*—a decisive, major battle against the U.S. Fleet.

Based on his analysis of numerous war gaming exercises against the U.S. Pacific Fleet, Yamamoto concluded that the Japanese Navy could never win an overwhelming victory at sea.

## Fact #35: April 1941—Admiral Osami Nagano Becomes Head of the IJN

Based on his experience in the United States, Nagano wanted to avoid war with America and hoped to persuade the Imperial Japanese Army to invade and secure the oil fields of the Dutch East Indies (now Indonesia) and Malaya (now Malaysia). Instead, the Army invaded China and embarked on a war that nearly depleted Japan's treasury.

In April, 1941, Nagano became Chief of the General Staff, making him the most senior officer in the Imperial Japanese Navy. By that time, Nagano had realized that the IJN had few remaining options if military conflict expanded outside China.

## Fact #36: July 1941—U.S. Freezes Japan's Assets in America

On July 24, 1941, Japanese troops landed at Camranh Bay in French Indochina (now Vietnam). In response, on July 26, 1941, the American government froze Japan's U.S.-held assets. The immediate response was the collapse of the foreign exchange market for Japanese yen. In effect, this meant that the Japanese government could not finance any of its import purchases for energy, raw materials for military equipment production, or chemicals for food production.

British Minister Oliver Lyttleton, a member of Winston Churchill's war cabinet, said this would surely provoke Japan to go to war.

Great Britain, which stood alone in the fight against Nazi Germany, saw this as a hopeful sign that the U.S. would soon enter the European conflict.

## Fact #37: July 1941—U.S. Embargo on Oil to Japan

Policy makers, who had successfully urged and implemented an oil embargo on Japan, thought the embargo would bankrupt Japan by 1942. Japan relied on the U.S. for 80 percent of its oil imports, and its military leaders knew that their war efforts would come to a standstill within a few years.

It turns out that the Office of Naval Intelligence underestimated Japan's oil inventory and may have gambled that Japan would initiate a withdrawal of troops from China rather than decide on a course of war.

Admiral Richmond Turner, then Director of War Plans, said that the oil embargo would trigger war.

Admiral Nagano later called World War II "the black war" because he believed the central issue was access to oil.

## Fact #38: August 1941—Isolationism is Alive and Well in America

In anticipation of involvement in the European conflict, Congress passed the Selective Training and Service Act in September, 1940. This was the first peacetime conscription law enacted in America's history. Men between the ages of 21 and 35 were required to register with local draft boards.

The law authorized the draft for one year. During the summer of 1941, President Roosevelt asked the U.S. Congress to extend the term of duty for the draftees beyond twelve months. On August 12th, the House of Representatives approved the extension by a single vote, 203-202. The vote was largely along party lines with 182 Democrats and 21 Republicans in favor and 65 Democrats, 133 Republicans, and 4 others against.

Japan's political and military leaders obviously did not think that this particular vote was significant or ignored it as a sign of the depth of isolationist sentiment in the U.S.

## Fact #39: October 1941—Yamamoto's View of Expanding the War Outside China

Based on his knowledge of the industrial might of the U.S., Yamamoto was against starting a war with America. In a letter dated October 24, 1941 from Yamamoto to Navy Minister Shigetaro Shimada, Yamamoto wrote:

"...Even more risky and illogical...is the idea of going to war against America, Britain and China after four years of exhausting operations in China and with the possibility of fighting Russia and having, moreover, to sustain ourselves unassisted for ten years or more in a protracted war over an area several times more vast than the European war theater. War with America and Britain should be avoided in light of the overall situation, and every effort should, of course, be made to that end."

Despite his strong reservations, months earlier Yamamoto had ordered his staff to prepare plans to attack the U.S. Fleet at Pearl Harbor.

## Fact #40: Nagano's View of the Plan to Attack Pearl Harbor

When he became Chief of the General Staff in 1941, Nagano was against Yamamoto's plan to attack Pearl Harbor. However, he relented when Yamamoto threatened to resign if the Navy did not accept his plan.

## Fact #41: Very Different Assessments of the Asset Freeze

Most U.S. policy makers and economic advisors believed that the embargo would result in the collapse of Japan's military government. Only Ambassador Joseph Grew, who ended up spending ten years in Japan, doubted that prevailing free-market economic theories applied to Japan. He believed that Japan was already a state-run economy and that the country was on a near-term path to starvation in order to support its war machine.

On the other side of the Pacific, the Cabinet Planning Board decided that Japan would quickly become "pauperized" and that the country must decide on a strategy for self-preservation. That strategy was war.

## Fact #42: North vs. South

Japan's Kwantung Army had been in Manchuria since 1931 and hoped for a chance to engage with its long-term Russian rivals across the border. In 1939, the two forces clashed in Mongolia, and the Soviet Army ripped Japan's Sixth Army to shreds. Some historians estimate that close to 45,000 IJA troops were killed, while the Soviets lost 8,000 soldiers.

This major setback weighed heavily on the leaders of the IJA because of troop commitments required to contain the Soviets in the north, to maintain control in Manchukuo and China, and to launch an offensive in the south.

## Fact #43: Germany Attacks the Soviet Union

On June 22, 1941, Germany violated the Nazi-Soviet Non-Aggression Pact and invaded the Soviet Union. The majority of the Soviet's Eastern Army was moved to the European front. This freed Japan from maintaining additional troops in Manchukuo and allowed them to prepare for the invasion of Southeast Asia.

## Fact #44: IJN Moves from War Gaming to War Planning

In 1941, Commander Shigeshi Uchida, Operations Section of the Naval General Staff, was in charge of planning for operations against the U.S. Pacific and Asiatic Fleets and the Dutch in Sumatra.

Uchida's diary entries of July 28th and 29th noted that the U.S. freeze caused the Japanese to give up their plan to attack the Soviets in the north. Instead, they would devote all their energies to invading the resource-rich southern regions. Furthermore, the planning staff projected a date for the outbreak of war as October 15th.

## Fact #45: The Decision to Attack on December 7$^{th}$ Amid Continuing Diplomatic Efforts for Peace

During September, the Naval General Staff (NGS) and the Navy Ministry conducted war games pitting the Japanese Navy against the U.S., British and Dutch forces. Uchida recommended that the attack should be scheduled for a Sunday. In his duty book entry dated October 21st, he noted:

"The NGS orders and directives to be sent out prior to the outbreak of war were discussed and decided. They were all drafted by me. It is expected that we are going to war on 8 December [7 December Hawaii Standard Time]."

However, on the diplomatic front, Foreign Minister Shigenori Togo was still trying to persuade his fellow Cabinet members to avoid war with the West—especially the United States.

In 1937, Togo was Japan's Ambassador to Germany, but he disliked the Nazis intensely. He was replaced after only ten months at the Germans' request by the embassy's military attaché, who was an admirer of the Third Reich. Togo was subsequently appointed Ambassador to the Soviet Union (1938-1940).

When General Hideki Tojo became Prime Minister in October, 1941, he asked Togo to become his Foreign Minister. Togo said that he would accept on one condition: the Cabinet must agree to negotiations with the U.S. on Japan's military operations in China. Tojo agreed.

However, the previous Cabinet had approved the IJA's invasion of French Indochina (now Vietnam). In retaliation, the U.S. froze Japan's assets and embargoed all exports of oil to Japan. Realistically, Japan and the U.S. were on an unavoidable collision course.

According to his grandson and author of his grandfather's biography, Shigehiko Togo wrote that the Foreign Minister's "real opponent was not the United States but the Japanese military." Despite opposition from the military, Togo pressed on with negotiations. He drafted two proposals for the United States: under Proposal A, Japanese troops would be withdrawn within 25 years (a compromise between his initial proposal of two-to-five years and the IJA's counter-proposal of 99 years); and under Proposal B, he proposed the immediate withdrawal of IJA troops from French Indochina in exchange for the termination of U.S. aid to the Chinese Nationalists and the resumption of oil exports to Japan.

These were sent to the Japanese Embassy in Washington for the final negotiations with Secretary of State Cordell Hull. Togo asserted that there was a translation error when the American side decoded the telegram and gave wrong information about the Japanese plan. In his memoirs, Hull wrote that the terms of Proposal B were "of so preposterous a character that no American official could ever have dreamed of accepting them."

The final step towards war came on November 26, 1941, when Hull demanded that Japan withdraw "all military naval, air and police forces from China and from Indochina"—conditions which the Secretary of State knew were totally unacceptable to the Imperial Japanese Government.

Shigehiko Togo recalled that his mother, Ise—the Foreign Minister's daughter—told him repeatedly of her vivid memory of the evening of November 27, 1941: "Your grandfather struggled so hard against the Japanese Army and the United States, trying to persuade both sides to prevent war. But when he returned home that evening, he was completely drained...because of Hull's rejection of peace; and the atmosphere in our family was so gloomy from that day on."

Foreign Minister Togo failed to prevent the war between Japan and the U.S., but he decided to remain a member of the Cabinet, first, to begin the war properly and, second, to end it as soon as possible.

Togo was removed from the Cabinet in late 1942 because of his on-going confrontation with Tojo. The Foreign Minister kept stating that Japan had to consider and respect the issue of the independence of the Southeast Asian countries which Japan had occupied. He would become Foreign Minister again in 1945 when it was clear that Japan was losing the war—this time to end it.

[Author's Note: Foreign Minister Togo was married to a German national and had one child, a daughter, Ise. At their first meeting, the author asked Shigehiko if his family was related to Admiral Heihachiro Togo, victor of the famous Battle of Tsushima and hero of the Russo-Japan War. The answer was, "No." The Foreign Minister's family was of Korean descent. Their ancestor had been kidnapped from Korea by warlord Hideyoshi Toyotomi's troops in the 1590s because of his unique skills at making pottery and ceramic glazes. Shigehiko's great-grandfather purchased the surname, Togo, from a financially distressed *samurai*.

Ise Togo was married to Fumihiko—subsequently adopted by Shigenori in order to perpetuate the family name and who later became the Japanese Ambassador to Washington during the Ford and Carter administrations. Ise and Fumihiko's son, Kazuhiko, is a retired senior Foreign Ministry official and an expert on Japan's relationship with Russia; Shigehiko, his twin brother, is a retired Washington Post journalist, author, and is currently fulfilling his course requirements for his PhD in religious studies.]

## Fact #46: "Success or Failure Depends on Refueling at Sea"

Rear Admiral Ryunosuke Kusaka was the Chief of Staff under Admiral Chuichi Nagumo in early 1941. He was fully aware that the success of an attack on Pearl Harbor would depend on the IJN's ability to refuel the Carrier Task Force on the long voyage from Japan to Hawaii.

Kusaka developed and implemented the protocol that the oil tanker should approach the ship needing fuel and not the other way around. He also established that of the two types of re-fueling positions—astern and alongside—alongside would be easier and result in fewer collision accidents.

## Fact #47: Selection of Lieutenant Commanders Minoru Genda and Mitsuo Fuchida

Kusaka persuaded the IJN's decision-makers to appoint Lieutenant Commander Minoru Genda as head of planning for the Pearl Harbor air strike and Lieutenant Commander Mitsuo Fuchida as head of training and leader of the attack force.

After the war, Genda said this about Fuchida, his classmate at the Japanese Naval Academy:

"Fuchida had a very strong fighting spirit—his best quality. He was also a gifted leader with the ability to understand any given situation and to react to it quickly. He was not only our best flight leader but a good staff man as well...cooperative with a clear head. The success of the Pearl Harbor attack depended upon the character and ability of its flight leader, and that is why Fuchida was selected for the job."

## Fact #48: November 1941—Fuchida as Leader

In early November, at their secret training site in Hitokappu Bay in northern Japan, Fuchida requested 40 live torpedoes for final practice for his pilots. Fleet Command Center said that supplies for the actual attack were limited, so they requisitioned only three torpedoes.

Fuchida and his torpedo squadron leader, Lieutenant Shigeharu "Bussan" Murata, selected three pilots with proven skill levels—first, second and third grade. The first and second grade pilots hit their target; the third grade pilot, as expected, missed.

Murata was heart-broken and wanted to cry. After they landed their observation plane, Fuchida tapped Murata on the shoulder and told him the following story:

"Look, Bussan. A long time ago, on the occasion of the Battle of Ichi-no-Tani, [General] Yoshitsune Minamoto approached a pass that appeared too steep for horses to descend. He asked the guide if he had ever seen horses coming down the hills. The guide said no, but he had seen deer going down. The General said, 'Both horses and deer have four legs,' and he kicked two horses downhill. One fell, but the other went down safely. He looked back at his soldiers and said, 'If half of you should reach the enemy, the victory is ours. Follow me!'"

Fuchida continued. "The battle ended in total victory for Yoshitsune. His chance of victory was one in two. Our chances are two out of three. If two-thirds of our 40 torpedoes should make it through, that makes 27 hits. Bussan, it's 'You guys, follow me!'"

Murata's dejected expression gave way to a smile. According to materials later published by the U.S. military, on December 7th, 27 of his squadron's torpedoes hit their targets.

[Author's Note: In the movie, *Tora, Tora, Tora*, Fuchida was portrayed as an outgoing jokester. He attended the world-wide premiere of the movie in New York in 1970 with his son and American-born daughter-in-law, Marie, who asked him if he minded being portrayed that way. Fuchida, who worked on the movie as a consultant, answered that he had to behave that way with his pilots to keep their spirits up; none thought they would return alive.]

## Fact #49: Yamamoto's Plan and Decision to Attack Pearl Harbor

One of the reasons Yamamoto was named Commander in Chief of the Combined Fleet was that it was widely believed that IJA extremists planned to assassinate him because of his opposition to expanding the war—especially against the U.S. The admiral's command position put him out to sea, on board the *Nagato*, and reduced the risk of his assassination.

The Japanese government decided on all-out war. Yamamoto saw almost no hope of success if the IJN relied on traditional battle strategies. "The most important thing to do in a war with the U.S.," Yamamoto firmly believed, "is to fiercely attack and destroy the U.S. main fleet at the outset of the war, so that the morale of the U.S. Navy and her people goes down to such an extent that it cannot be recovered."

## Fact #50: Assessment of a Prolonged War

H.P. Wilmott, the well-known World War II historian, concluded that, short of a negotiated peace treaty in the first two years after the attack on Pearl Harbor, Japan could not possibly achieve victory against the Americans.

Even at its peak, Japanese production capacity was only 10 percent of potential U.S. output. Unless the IJN could engineer a decisive battle and destroy the U.S. Pacific Fleet within two years, Japan faced a war of attrition that it could not win.

## Fact #51: Dissension within the IJN

Rear Admiral Tamon Yamaguchi graduated from the Japanese Naval Academy and studied at Princeton University for two years. In 1941, when he was told that planners had decided not to include his 2nd Carrier Division in the Pearl Harbor attack, he got drunk and beat his superior officer, Admiral Nagumo. Officers who were at the fight did not intervene, and Nagumo agreed to include the 2nd Air Carrier Division as part of the Task Force.

Yamaguchi was never court-martialed for this incident. He went down with his ship at the Battle of Midway.

## Fact #52: November 23, 1941—Nagumo's Operations Order No. 1

In his Operations Order No. 1 to the Carrier Task Force, Admiral Nagumo wrote: "The initial air attack is scheduled at 0330 hours [8 AM Hawaii Standard Time]. Upon completion of the air attacks, the Task Force will immediately withdraw and return to Japan..."

Nagumo was a specialist in torpedo and surface tactics, and he had limited experience with naval aviation. He was appointed

Commander in Chief largely because of his seniority. His critics within the IJN argued that he had become more cautious and less aggressive as he grew older. In his Operations Order No. I, Nagumo did not clearly state what "completion of the air attacks" meant.

## Fact #53: November 23, 1941—Nagumo's Operations Order No. 3

In Operations Order No. 3, Nagumo wrote: "After the launching of the second attack units is completed, the Task Force will withdraw northward at a speed of about 24 knots. The first attack units are scheduled to return between 0530 [1000 Hawaii Standard Time] and 0600 [1030 Hawaii Standard Time] hours and the second attack units are scheduled to return between 0645 [1115 Hawaii Standard Time] and 0715 [1145 Hawaii Standard Time] hours."

"Immediately after the return of the first and second attack units, preparations for the next attack will be completed. At this time, carrier attack planes capable of carrying torpedoes will be armed with such as long as the supply lasts."

## Fact #54: Communications Security Measures

After Hitokappu Bay—then in northern Japan and since the end of the Pacific War under Russian control—was chosen for attack training, Kusaka ordered air bases at Kagoshima on Kyushu to continue mock flight training exercises. He also ordered ships in southern Japan to send out frequent false wireless messages. The objective was to mislead the Americans into thinking that the Carrier Task Force was still in the south at Bungo Strait.

On the other side of the Pacific, the Office of U.S. Navy intelligence lost all trace of the whereabouts of the Task Force.

## Fact #55: Heading Off to War

On November 26th, just before sunrise, the Task Force Fleet departed Hitokappu Bay. Initially the seas were rough, pitching ships 25 degrees or more, but the weather turned calm after several days.

As oil refueling was the top priority, no provision had been made for water re-supply during the trip to Pearl Harbor. The fleet carried only 44 tons of water, equivalent to 1.5 tons a day for the duration of the voyage, so that water was used sparingly for cooking, washing faces every morning and hands after work and before meals.

## Fact #56: December 1, 1941—Japan's Final Decision to Use Armed Force

On December 1st, according to the diary of Commander Sadamu Sanagi, Operations Section of the Naval General Staff, a conference of the key government leaders was held with the Emperor. An Imperial Order was issued directing the use of armed force.

## Fact #57: Strict Radio Silence

According to IJN war documents, the Task Force Fleet maintained and enforced absolute radio silence. Telegraph keys were removed and secured under lock and key. This fact undermines revisionist claims that President Roosevelt knew about the impending attack.

## Fact #58: December 7th—"A Date That Will Live in Infamy"

The attack on Pearl Harbor began at 7:48 AM on December 7th, 1941, Hawaii Standard Time. This was 3:18 AM Japan Standard Time on December 8th.

From 1900 to 1947, the Territory of Hawaii had its own time zone—set at 5.5 hours behind Eastern Standard Time.

## Fact #59: Impact of Decision Not to Send a Third Wave to Attack Pearl Harbor

Admiral Nagumo's decision not to risk either his airplanes or his task force ships in a third attack wave meant that the critical oil tanks and repair facilities at Pearl Harbor were left largely intact. There is evidence that Yamamoto was not pleased with Nagumo's decision.

Storage tanks holding 4.5 million barrels of oil were not blown up. If they had been, the U.S. Pacific Fleet would have been forced back to the West Coast, and operations during the first year of the war would have been severely curtailed.

Moreover, as repair facilities were largely undamaged, many of the repairs were performed on site at Pearl Harbor and ships made sea-worthy again very quickly.

## Fact #60: Yamamoto's Opinion of Nagumo's Performance

Although the two air strikes inflicted terrible damage and loss of life on the Pacific Fleet, Yamamoto knew that his Task Force could have done more and believed that Nagumo should have ordered the third strike.

Fuchida, the leader of the attack, could not understand why the mini-submarine attack units were awarded Citations for

Outstanding Deed of Valor while his pilots were given lesser Citations for Prominent Deed of Valor. After the war ended, Fuchida wrote, "Now, I understood. As I suspected, Nagumo's intentions were not in line with those of his boss, Commander Yamamoto."

## Fact #61: Admirals Nagano and Yamamoto—Lessons Not Learned

During the many years each spent in the U.S., both Admirals Nagano and Yamamoto learned a great deal about America's industrial might and military strength. However, they did not learn enough about the psyche of the American people or what triggers could unite a politically divided U.S. —such as the sinking of the USS *Maine* that set off the Spanish-American War or of the *Lusitania* that tipped America away from isolationism and towards participation in World War I.

On December 8th, President Roosevelt delivered his "Date of Infamy" speech. Thirty-three minutes after he finished, the Congress declared war on Japan.

## Fact #62: News Control under the Public Security Preservation Laws

The Public Security Preservation Laws were amended in 1941, and the Japanese government suppressed any news that it regarded as potentially harmful to the morale of the Japanese people. News of the IJN's successful attack on Pearl Harbor was published immediately, but the defeat at Midway was not made public until the very end of the war.

## Fact #63: IJN Focus on Decisive Battle

The IJN's strategy centered on a decisive surface battle in the Western Pacific—and early in the war before the U.S. Navy had superiority in terms of fleet size and fire power. This did not happen.

With the defeat at Midway, IJN leaders realized too late that they had neglected on-going recruiting and training programs to replace killed or disabled fighter and bomber pilots.

Moreover, little thought had been given to logistics—to either protecting their own maritime fleet or destroying the enemy's communications lines.

## Fact #64: Conclusion—IJN's Decisive Battle Strategy

Admirals Nagano and Yamamoto knew that the IJN could be victorious only if they could "defeat" the Americans in a decisive battle during the first two or three years of a war.

Looking at the tremendous growth of American naval fire power between the start of the war and 1943, it is clear that Japan decided to start a war with the one country in the world it could not defeat.

By attacking Pearl Harbor, Japan moved the U.S. from its isolationist stance to mobilizing and uniting its people and industries to annihilate the enemy. The IJN's operational plan to engage the U.S. Pacific Fleet in a decisive battle and force a peace settlement was more wishful thinking than a realistic strategy.

## Fact #65: George Shuichi Mizota—Admiral Yamamoto's Interpreter

George Shuichi Mizota was born in Japan and immigrated to Redlands, California with his parents when he was nine years old.

He graduated from Stanford Law School in 1924. Aware that the recently enacted Federal Immigration Act would not open doors for him with prospective employers in America, he decided to move back to Japan.

Initially, he was employed as an interpreter at the Navy Ministry, but before long he became Admiral Isoroku Yamamoto's interpreter. Although Yamamoto spoke excellent English based on his years of studying at Harvard and working at the Japanese Embassy in Washington, DC, he reportedly relied on Mizota as his interpreter to give him extra time to think about what he was hearing and how to respond.

Mizota attended many important meetings, including the London Naval Conference of 1930 that set limits on the tonnage and construction of capital and auxiliary warships for the United Kingdom, the U.S., Japan, France and Italy. Mizota told his military employers that Japan could not defeat the U.S., so after the start of war, the Naval Ministry put him on paid leave.

In 1945, when it became clear that Japan was losing the war, Mizota was again asked to be an interpreter for the leaders of the IJN. He was with Japan's military and political representatives who flew from Tokyo to Manila in August to meet General Douglas MacArthur's staff to discuss Japan's surrender terms. And on September 2nd, he was on the USS *Missouri* as an interpreter for the Japanese delegation that accepted and signed the Surrender Treaty.

[Author's Note: The author first met Mizota at a Stanford alumni party in Tokyo in 1974. He remembers Mizota's stage actor's voice and diction—equally captivating in English and Japanese—as he talked about his experience with Admiral Yamamoto.]

## Fact #66: Role of Intelligence—IJN

The Japanese might have had intelligence indicating that the British could not defend Singapore. In November, 1940, the German cruiser *Atlantis* fired on the British cargo ship, *Automedon*, northwest of Sumatra. The Germans boarded the sinking ship and discovered top secret British papers stating that the U.K. could do little or nothing if the Japanese attacked Singapore and Siam (present-day Thailand).

The Germans gave the papers to the Japanese, who reportedly used this secret information to plan their attack on Singapore. The captain of the *Atlantis* was given a special *samurai* sword, one of only two Germans given such a high honor during World War II.

## Fact #67: Role of Intelligence—U.S. Navy

The U.S. intelligence agencies had broken Japanese diplomatic codes at the time of the Washington Naval Conference in 1921 and their military codes by 1941.

Bad luck and bad timing prevented information from deciphered codes—indicating an imminent attack on Pearl Harbor—from reaching the appropriate military and political leaders before the Japanese pilots had completed their two air strikes.

Even worse bad luck and timing for the Japanese were to follow. The encrypted cable declaring war from the Japanese government arrived at their embassy in Washington, D.C. on December 7th. Because it was a Sunday, no one was at the embassy. Ambassador Kichisaburo Nomura and Special Envoy Saburo Kurusu had to call in a junior diplomatic official, whose typing skills were limited to one-finger pecking, to prepare the memo for delivery to the U.S. government. Compounding this delay, Secretary of State Cordell

Hull's morning meeting ran late, so that he was unavailable to accept the declaration of war until after the attack on Pearl Harbor began—hence, the "sneak attack."

[Author's Note: Under Japan's code of *bushido*, a warrior is obligated to warn his opponent of an impending strike—even if it is one second before the assault. When the attack pilots learned of their government's diplomatic failure, they were plagued by guilt. In 2005, at a speech at the Foreign Correspondents Club in Tokyo, Zenji Abe, a surviving pilot, said he did not learn for many years about the failure to declare war before the attack had started. He said that this was a disgrace on Japan.]

**Fact #68: U.S. Fleet, Aircraft Carriers—1941 to 1943**

The attack on Pearl Harbor was dramatic evidence that the unchallenged supremacy of the battleship had been eclipsed by air power and the aircraft carrier. The U.S. Navy responded quickly.

On December 7, 1941, the U.S. fleet had 8 aircraft carriers. During 1943, as a result of the Two-Ocean Navy Act, the U.S. Navy added:

• 7 *Essex*-class carriers (capable of carrying 90-100 planes with a maximum cruising speed of 33 knots),
• 9 *Independence*-class carriers (capable of carrying 30-40 planes with a maximum cruising speed of 32 knots).

**Fact #69: U.S. Fleet—1941 to 1945**

During the 1,366 days between December 7, 1941 and Japan's surrender on September 2, 1945, the U.S. Navy added to its fleet:

- 6 battleships
- 21 fleet carriers
- 70 escort carriers
- 35 cruisers
- 206 destroyers
- 361 destroyer escorts
- 120 submarines
- 451 minesweepers
- 1,104 patrol boats
- 3,604 amphibious and auxiliary craft

**Fact #70: Submarine Warfare—Rules of Engagement at the Beginning of World War I**

At the start of World War I, submarines were a relatively new warfare technology. In fact, they were considered illegal weapons by the Allied countries.

In the event of a submarine attack on a merchant vessel, the rules of engagement called for the submarine captain to surface, warn the captain of the merchant vessel that his ship would be fired upon, and provide passage for the merchant crew to safe quarters.

The German U-boat command ignored these gentleman's rules and sank a number of British merchant vessels. The Allies considered this barbaric behavior. In May, 1915 a German U-boat sank the British passenger ship, *Lusitania*, killing 1,198 of the 1,959 people on board.

This was considered a horrific act of savagery and helped to change American minds about active participation in what they had considered previously to be a European war.

## Fact #71: IJN Submarine Fleet

Prior to the outbreak of war, most IJN admirals had been trained in traditional surface operations and tactics and believed in the supremacy of the battleship. Few had experience or knowledge of the submersible ship which the Germans had developed into a lethal torpedo launcher. Although IJN engineers had developed advanced designs, submarine construction received relatively small amounts of funding. In addition, various units of the IJN lobbied for different, mission-specific designs—so manufacturing costs remained high for low-volume production runs, and crew training and maintenance were never standardized.

The result was that the IJN deployed a limited number of submarines for reconnaissance and task force escort instead of for the sinking of U.S. supply ships.

## Fact #72: U.S. Navy and the New Age of Submarine Warfare

Although the submarine had been viewed as an illegal weapon, the devastating attack on Pearl Harbor and the ruthless deployment of German U-boats in the Atlantic over-rode the prior reluctance of the Americans to attack merchant ships with undersea torpedoes.

Captain Charles Lockwood, the Naval Attaché at the U.S. Embassy in London in early 1941, studied the German U-boat "wolf pack" operations which were destroying British merchant ships almost at will. During the first six months of 1942, U.S. merchant losses to the German U-boats in the Atlantic exceeded total merchant fleet losses during World War I.

Focusing on submarine strategy for the U.S. Navy, Lockwood became concerned that the radio communications required to coordinate a wolf pack and the emerging effectiveness of direction-finding technologies increased the risk of detection and destruction of submarines.

Based on his observations and analysis, Lockwood devised a "lone wolf" strategy. This required the wholesale replacement of submarine commanders with officers who were capable of making decisions on-the-spot without a chain of command.

Promoted to Vice Admiral in early 1943, Lockwood was Pacific Fleet Commander, Submarines from early 1943 until the end of the war. His forces sank close to one-third of all Japanese warships—eight aircraft carriers, one battleship and eleven cruisers.

Equally important, his submarines played a vital role in stopping shipments of oil and food from reaching Japan. They sank two-thirds of all Japanese merchant vessels—1,152 Japanese transport ships representing 56 percent of all Japanese merchant tonnage.

The U.S. lost 52 submarines, and the submarine fatality rate was the highest of all U.S. military units.

## Fact #73: The Red Menace

The major Allied countries were the U.S., Great Britain and the Soviet Union. All were focused on defeating, first, Nazi Germany and, second, Imperial Japan. However, the Allies had an uneasy relationship because the Western countries viewed the Soviet Union with suspicion and concern. The Soviets were a Communist country, whose values were in total opposition to the West's. Even Japan viewed the Soviet Union as an ideological threat separate from their bitter rivalry lingering from their 1905 war.

In this political atmosphere, Richard Sorge, a German journalist who had moved to Japan in 1933, developed an extensive network of military, political and journalistic sources. Working out of the German embassy, he gathered information about Japan's war plans.

In fact, Sorge was an intelligence officer for the Soviet Union. Through his network, he learned that Japan planned to attack the Dutch East Indies, French Indochina, and the British colonies in the south—but not the Soviet Union in the north. This allowed Stalin—who was concerned about fighting a two-front war—to re-deploy portions of his Eastern Army to the Western front in anticipation of Germany's violation of the Non-Aggression Treaty.

Many historians consider Sorge to be the real-life equal of the fictional James Bond in terms of his success. He was caught and executed in Japan before the end of the war.

In their excellent book, *Target Tokyo: The Story of the Sorge Spy Ring*, Gordon Prange, Donald Goldstein and Katherine Dillon provide all of the details of Sorge's intelligence exploits—coordinated largely within the German Embassy in Tokyo.

## Fact #74: The Russo-Japan War That Never Ended

Most historians writing about the Russo-Japan War focus on the famous Battle of Tsushima Straits. Little attention is given to the Battle of Mukden, which took place in March, 1905. The Imperial Japanese Army—with forces of 270,000 men—faced the Russian Imperial Army—with 330,000 men.

The Russians were defeated and suffered nearly 100,000 casualties, while the Japanese casualties were close to 75,000. Neither side ever forgot what the opposing side did to them. Mutual distrust and hatred had a definite impact on the events leading to the Soviet Union's declaration of war and invasion of Manchukuo in August, 1945. Stalin and his military leaders had anticipated another war with Japan for many years. At this time, the Japanese controlled Korea, and Koreans were considered subjects of Imperial Japan. Stalin, worried about possible pro-Japan support in his eastern provinces, ordered the removal of over 170,000 ethnic Koreans, who lived in the Russian Far East, to Soviet Central Asia, primarily present-day Kazakhstan.

It is interesting to note that the Far East Russian territories, now called Primorskii Krai, had been Chinese territory until 1858. Under the Treaty of Aigun (1858) and the Treaty of Peking (1860), Imperial Russia forced the weak Chinese government to hand over sovereignty.

[Author's Note: In Far East Russia, the museums in Khabarovsk and Komsomolsk-on-Amur have large murals depicting the 150th anniversary of the signing of the Treaty of Aigun. The paintings show two Russian military officers standing behind two seated Chinese officials who are signing the treaty documents.

In Kazakhstan, ethnic Koreans who are descendants of the forced migrants generally do not speak Korean. They still recount stories of how their grandparents were forcibly moved in cattle cars from the Russian Far East on the Pacific to Central Asia.

As a group, Korean-Kazakhstanis are a well-educated, prosperous segment of their national society, and they are featured in the histories and cultural lore of the new republic. A recent government-funded film depicting the forced migration highlights the generosity of local families who took in the strange-looking immigrants and helped them to build their homes when spring arrived.

The film premiere was attended by the South Korean Ambassador to Kazakhstan and the President of Kazakhstan's

Federal Senate, who is an ethnic Korean and a key advisor to Nursultan Nazarbayev, Kazakhstan's President-for-Life. At the small banquet that followed, several of the ethnic Koreans gave beautiful presentations of famous Russian poetry or literature. Even at a celebration of the independent Republic of Kazakhstan, the influence of Russia and the former Soviet Union were on clear display.]

## Fact #75: February 1945—Nagano Relieved as Head of IJN

In February 1945, when it became clear that Japan was facing defeat, Japan's war cabinet dismissed Nagano as the IJN's Chief of Staff. After Japan surrendered, he was designated a Class A War Criminal and was tried at the Tokyo War Crimes Trial. However, he died in 1947 while in prison and before the trial ended.

## Fact #76: February 1945—Secret Accord at Yalta

On the other side of the world, it was clear that the Allies would defeat Nazi Germany, and President Roosevelt, Prime Minister Winston Churchill and Premier Josef Stalin met in Yalta, Russia. On February 11th, Stalin secretly confirmed that the Soviet Army would enter the war against Japan provided that "the former rights of Russia violated by the treacherous attack of Japan in 1904" were restored.

After Japan's victory in 1905, the IJA stayed on Soviet soil until 1927. They continued to pose a threat to Soviet sovereignty with their 1931 invasion of Manchuria, just south of the Russian border.

Stalin's message was clear about his intention to claim territory that Russia was forced to cede in 1905.

## Fact #77: March 9-10, 1945—Firebombing of Tokyo

On the evening of March 9-10, 1945, 334 American B-29s took off towards Tokyo; 279 of them dropped approximately 1,700 tons of incendiary bombs, destroying 16 square miles of the city within hours. An estimated 88,000 to 100,000 people—mainly civilians—died in the resulting firestorm. This was more than the estimated immediate deaths resulting from either of the atomic bombs dropped on Hiroshima and Nagasaki.

The U.S. Strategic Bombing Survey later estimated that a million people were injured and a million residents lost their homes. This bombing raid was larger than the Allied fire-bombing of Dresden.

In *The Gods of Heavenly Punishment*—published on March 10, 2013—Jennifer Cody Epstein weaves stories about Japanese, American and European men and women who are swept into the devastation of the Pacific War. She writes about the operational planning for and precision bombing over Tokyo that inflicted suffering, death and destruction on an unprecedented scale.

Japan was unable to defend against this attack, and the military leaders knew that they were staring into the abyss of total defeat.

## Fact #78: May, 1945—The Beginning of the End and Shigenori Togo's Role

Taking the responsibility for Japan's defeat in the Pacific War, Tojo resigned from the Prime Minister's office in July, 1944. Tojo was replaced by General Kuniaki Koiso, who resigned after less than a year. In April 1945, Admiral Kantaro Suzuki—regarded as a loyal and trusted servant of the Emperor Showa—was appointed as Prime Minister. Suzuki asked Shigenori Togo, the Foreign Minister at the beginning of the war, to take that post for a second time. Togo told Suzuki that he would accept the position only if he were allowed to pursue peace negotiations with the United States. The Prime Minister agreed, and Togo was once again Japan's Foreign Minister—this time to end the war.

On May 8th, Nazi Germany surrendered. A few days later, Togo sent a secret cable to Ambassador Naotake Sato in Moscow: "...and once the enemy's European air forces are transferred to the Pacific, we will encounter unimaginable destructive power, and we may be facing the same fate that led to the downfall of Hitler's Germany."

Togo tried to seek peace talks by negotiating via the Soviet Union, because that was the only channel agreeable to the Imperial Japanese Army.

In mid-May, Japan's top six leaders—the Prime Minister, Foreign Minister, Ministers of the Army and the Navy, and the Chiefs of Staff of the Army and the Navy—began a series of secret meetings at the Imperial Palace to discuss how to end the war.

## Fact #79: July 12, 1945—Togo's Secret Quest for Peace

In July, Togo sent a cable to Ambassador Sato in Moscow: "We are now secretly giving consideration to the termination of the war because of the pressing situation which confronts Japan both at home and abroad."

"His Majesty the Emperor, mindful of the fact that the present war daily brings greater evil and sacrifice upon the peoples of all belligerent powers, desires from his heart that it may be quickly terminated."

In his memoirs, *The Cause for Japan*, written during his postwar imprisonment, Togo wrote that he indicated that Japan conveyed to the Allies that Japan would agree to unconditional surrender as far as the armed forces were concerned—but not the Japanese nation.

Togo maintained that the Big Three Leaders ignored this offer to discuss peace at Potsdam.

## Fact #80: Stalin and Truman at the Potsdam Conference

At the Potsdam Conference in occupied Germany, Stalin told President Harry Truman that the Soviets would enter the war against Japan on August 15th. In his private diary—published in 1980—Truman wrote: "Fini Japs when that comes about."

## Fact #81: August 2, 1945—Seeking Surrender Help from the Russians

At the beginning of August, Togo again cabled a secret message—intercepted and deciphered by MAGIC—to Sato: "At present, in accordance with the Imperial will, there is a unanimous determination to seek the good offices of the Russians in ending the war."

Several historians have commented that, given the long-standing hostility between Japan and Russia, it is strange that Togo—who had been Ambassador in Moscow—used the Soviets as an intermediary.

## Fact #82: U.S. Debate about the Atomic Bomb

Some American war planners estimated that the final push to defeat Japan—an invasion of Japan itself—would result in 500,000 Allied casualties. Others thought that this estimate was too high given that during the war to mid-1945, military casualties were lower than this for the entire rest of the world.

In his private diary, Truman wrote on June 17th: "I have to decide Japanese strategy—shall we invade Japan proper or shall we bomb and blockade? That is my hardest decision to date. But I'll make it when I have all the facts."

In August, 1945, President Truman decided to use America's secret weapon, the atomic bomb, to end the war with Japan. Submarine Commander Lockwood and his immediate superior, Fleet Admiral Nimitz, believed that Japan was already defeated and could be compelled to surrender with a tightening of the submarine blockade—stopping all food supplies and oil from entering Japan.

MacArthur and Eisenhower were also against using the atomic bomb for ethical reasons. Whether Truman took MacArthur's opinion seriously is not clear. In his private diary, he wrote: "We discussed Mr. Prima Donna...Five Star MacArthur. He's worse than the Cabots and the Lodges—they at least talked with one another before they told God what to do. Mac tells God right off...I don't see why in Hell Roosevelt didn't order Wainwright home and let MacArthur be a martyr."

The President, as Commander in Chief, gave the order to drop the bomb, and Hiroshima was destroyed on August 6th.

## Fact #83: The End

The Soviets declared war on Japan on August 8th, the Americans dropped the second atomic bomb on the 9th and, on the 15th, Emperor Hirohito told his subjects in a recorded speech broadcast over the radio that Japan would terminate the nation's war effort.

## Fact #84: The Casualties

It is impossible to determine the exact number of casualties in the Pacific War. However, official estimates indicate that the number of deaths was:

- Americans—52,000
- Japanese Military—1,140,500
- Japanese Civilians—700,000 to 1,000,000

About 24.2 percent of Japanese soldiers and 19.7 percent of Japanese sailors died during the Pacific War. This compared with 3.7 percent of U.S. Marines, 2.5 percent of U.S. soldiers, and 1.5 percent of U.S. sailors.

## Fact #85: Mutiny at Atsugi

General Douglas MacArthur, Supreme Commander of Allied Occupation Forces, was scheduled to land at Atsugi Base near Yokohama on August 30th. Unknown to the Americans, Captain Yasuna Kozono, Commander of the 302nd Naval Air Corps, had seized control of the air base following the Emperor's surrender speech on August 15th.

Kozono threatened to carry on the war with his fighter pilots in order to preserve the Japanese nation. Several admirals tried to persuade Kozono to step down, but he refused. On August 24th, Captain Mitsuo Fuchida, leader of the attack on Pearl Harbor, headed to Atsugi Base. The guards at the gate recognized the national hero and allowed Fuchida to drive past the manned machine guns.

Fuchida knew Kozono from their days together at the Japanese Naval Academy, and the two sat down to talk about the coming surrender. Kozono had not slept for days, and Fuchida and several others overpowered the leader of the mutiny. Six Zero pilots ran to their planes and flew off, but they surrendered after landing at a nearby IJA air base.

The mutiny ended, and MacArthur landed at Atsugi as scheduled on August 30th. This was followed by the signing of the surrender treaty, which took place in Tokyo Bay on September 2nd on the deck of the USS *Missouri.*

**Fact #86: General Tomoyuki Yamashita**

Starting on December 8, 1941 [December 7th, Hawaii Standard Time], Yamashita moved south with his 30,000 troops from French Indochina (now Vietnam) towards the British colonies of Malaya (now Malaysia) and Singapore. To get through the tropical jungles, they abandoned their trucks and rode on bicycles.

The British had ruled out an attack from the north—because, according to a British officer, "we wouldn't do it that way." By the time Yamashita's troops reached Singapore in early February, the British had all of their large artillery guns pointed south—in the wrong direction.

On February 15, 1942, Yamashita—whose troops had surrounded the city—called for a surrender conference with General Arthur Percival. Yamashita demanded that the British surrender by 6 PM that evening. Percival insisted on 8 AM the following morning. Yamashita knew that if he agreed to a surrender the following day, the British would send out scouts, discover that they outnumbered the IJA by three-to-one, and counter-attack and annihilate Yamashita's troops. He insisted on surrender at "6 PM, today."

Yamashita's interpreter, Masakatsu Hamamoto, a totally bilingual Harvard College graduate, was in Tokyo during this campaign. Within a few seconds after listening to an English speaker,

Hamamoto could tell Yamashita what the speaker said and did not say. At the surrender negotiation, Yamashita's temporary interpreter was not as fluent as Hamamoto. He took a long time questioning Percival for clarification. Yamashita, impatient for an answer from Percival, lost his temper and shouted, "Surrender—yes or no!"

This shocked Percival, and he agreed to surrender at 6 PM. Yamashita's 30,000 troops had captured over 100,000 British and Commonwealth soldiers. He became known as the Tiger of Malaya.

After the war was over, it was revealed that Prime Minister Winston Churchill delivered a secret speech to Parliament in April, 1942 about the surrender of 100,000 Commonwealth soldiers to 30,000 Japanese. He was dismayed that so many were captured by so few, and he cautioned against making this news available to the public.

After the surrender of Singapore, IJA troops were involved in a massacre of civilians. Yamashita ordered the execution of the officer and troops who were involved. There is no evidence of a link to this disciplinary action, but Yamashita was relieved of his command and sent to Manchukuo until late in the war.

In the final months of the war, Japan was desperate for Yamashita's proven leadership. He was ordered to the Philippines to regroup IJA forces that had no air cover, were on severely inadequate food rations, and were short on ammunition. He moved the vast majority of his several hundred thousand troops out of Manila to take defensive positions. Approximately 4,000 IJA soldiers remained in Manila alongside 15,000 IJN marines under the command of Rear Admiral Sanji Iwabuchi. Iwabuchi—whose chain of command was to the IJN and not to Yamashita—was ordered to defend at all costs against landing American troops. The ensuing violence resulted in the deaths of approximately 100,000 civilians.

After Japan's surrender, Yamashita was arrested and tried by a U.S. military tribunal for the Manila Massacre. MacArthur personally chose the military judges. None had legal or previous trial experience, and a great deal of hearsay was admitted into evidence—in violation of American legal principles. However, evidence that indicated that Yamashita had nothing to do with the massacre was ruled inadmissible by the military judges.

On December 7, 1945, Yamashita was sentenced to death for "command responsibility." Yamashita's defense team—comprised of U.S. Army lawyers—appealed the verdict, first, to the Philippines Supreme Court and, second, to the U.S. Supreme Court, but both declined to review the verdict. Yamashita was hanged in February, 1946.

The U.S. Supreme Court has never overturned the Yamashita decision, which holds that a commander can be held accountable for crimes committed by his troops even if he did not issue the orders, did not know about them, or did not have the means to stop them.

This so-called Yamashita Standard has not been applied by the U.S. military since 1946.

[Author's Note: In 1949, A. Frank Reel, one of Yamashita's defense lawyers, published *The Case of General Yamashita*. His account, which reads like a John Grisham novel, provides a summary of the military commission's proceedings and an assessment of the trial's key issues and participants, particularly of Yamashita. In *Yamashita's Ghost*, published in 2012, Allan Ryan—who clerked for Supreme Court Justice Byron White and was a U.S. Marine Corps judge advocate— provides a riveting and meticulous analysis in layman's terms of the trial's proceedings and key legal issues and why the Yamashita Standard is so relevant to the armed conflicts we face today.]

## Fact #87: International Military Tribunal for the Far East

On January 19, 1946, General MacArthur, Supreme Commander of the Allied Powers, established the International Military Tribunal for the Far East (IMTFE). Its objective was to prosecute the Japanese politicians and military leaders responsible for starting and waging war against the Allied nations.

## Fact #88: The Tokyo War Crimes Trial

The most prominent war criminals were tried at the Tokyo War Crimes Trial.

As many as 50 suspects—such as Nobusuke Kishi, who later became Prime Minister, and Yoshisuke Aikawa, founder and head of Nissan—were charged but released in 1947 and 1948.

There remained 29 defendants—all designated as Class A War Criminals. Chief among those named and prosecuted were:

Government Officials

- Koki Hirota, Prime Minister (1936-1937), Foreign Minister (1933-1936, 1937-1938)
- Baron Kiichiro Hiranuma, Prime Minister (1939), President of the Privy Council
- Naoki Hoshino, Chief Cabinet Secretary
- Marquis Koichi Kido, Lord Keeper of the Privy Seal
- Toshio Shiratori, Ambassador to Italy
- Shigenori Togo, Foreign Minister (1941-1942, 1945)
- Mamoru Shigemitsu, Foreign Minister (1943-1945)
- Okinori Kaya, Finance Minister (1941-1944)
- Yosuke Matsuoka, Foreign Minister (1940-1941)

Military Officers

- General Hideki Tojo, Prime Minister (1941-1944),
  War Minister (1940-1941)
- General Seishiro Itagaki, War Minister (1938-1939)
- General Sadao Araki, War Minister (1931-1934)
- Field Marshal Shunroku Hata, War Minister (1939-1940)
- Admiral Shigetaro Shimada, Navy Minister (1941-1944)
- General Kenryo Sato, Chief of the Military Affairs Bureau
- General Kuniaki Koiso, Prime Minister (1944-1945),
  Governor General of Korea (1942-1944)
- Admiral Takazumi Oka, Chief of the Bureau of Naval Affairs
- Lieutenant General Hiroshi Oshima, Ambassador to Germany
- Admiral Osami Nagano, Navy Minister (1936-1937), Chief
  of the Imperial Japanese Navy General Staff (1941-1944)
- General Jiro Minami, Governor-General of Korea (1936-1942)
- General Kenji Doihara, Chief of the Intelligence
  Service in Manchukuo
- General Heitaro Kimura, Commander of the Burma Area Army
- General Iwane Matsui, Commander of the Shanghai Expeditionary
  Force and Central China Area Army
- Lieutenant General Akira Muto, Chief of Staff of the 14th Area
  Army
- Colonel Kingoro Hashimoto, Founder of Sakurakai (IJA
  Ultranationalist Faction)
- General Yoshijiro Umezu, Commander of the Kwantung Army,
  Chief of the Imperial Japanese Army General Staff Office
  (1944-1945)
- Lieutenant General Teiichi Suzuki, Chief of the Cabinet Planning
  Board

Civilian Defendant

• Shumei Okawa, Political Philosopher and Pro-War Faction Leader

**Fact #89: Exclusion of the Emperor from the War Crimes Trial**

As early as November 26, 1945, MacArthur indicated that the Emperor's abdication would not be necessary. In large part due to the fear that the Soviets would attempt to export Communism to the shores of Japan, the U.S. believed that rebuilding an anti-Communist nation would be less difficult if the Emperor were retained under a new constitution. They worked not only to prevent the Imperial family from being indicted but also to ensure that the defendants did not provide testimony that implicated the Emperor in wartime activities.

According to several historians, Brigadier General Bonner Fellers played a major role in coordinating the testimonies that the key war defendants would give at the Tokyo War Crimes Trial. In *Embracing Defeat*, which was awarded the Pulitzer Prize, John Dower, provides the details of how the government leaders in Washington, D.C. and the U.S. military leaders in Tokyo crafted and implemented their plan to avoid naming the Emperor as a war criminal—in order to maintain stability during the period of reconstruction.

[Author's Note: In early 2013, the author talked to Yoko Narahashi, Japan casting director for *The Last Samurai*. She is a co-producer of *The Emperor*, a film which tells the story of how MacArthur and Fellers worked to exclude the Emperor from being indicted as a war criminal. Her grandfather, Teizaburo Sekiya, was the Vice Minister of the Imperial Household Ministry before the Pacific War; after the war, he was an Advisory Officer to the Privy Council. He played a significant role in setting up the first meeting between the Emperor and MacArthur and is portrayed in *The Emperor*.]

## Fact #90: Lawyers to Defend Japanese War Criminals

The war crimes defendants were represented by over a hundred attorneys, seventy-five percent Japanese and twenty-five percent American, plus a support staff.

The defense opened its case on January 27, 1947, and finished its presentation 225 days later. A major problem throughout the trial was the shortage of interpreters—and an even more acute shortage of interpreters who understood Japanese and Anglo-Saxon legal terms.

## Fact #91: John Gregory Brannon—Defense Counsel at the Tokyo War Crimes Trial

John Brannon was an American attorney from Kansas City, Missouri. Sensing an opportunity to be a front-line participant in a major historical event, he applied for a position as a defense lawyer at the Tokyo War Crimes Trial. He arrived in Tokyo on May 17, 1946 and was appointed by MacArthur to defend three Class A War Criminals:

• Osami Nagano, Chief of the Imperial Japanese Navy General Staff,
• Shigetaro Shimada, Navy Minister, and
• Takazumi Oka, Chief of the Bureau of Naval Affairs

Later in the trial, Brannon also took over as defense counsel for:

• General Kenryo Sato, Chief of the Military Affairs Bureau

In a letter dated November 25, 1947 to his brother Bernard, he wrote: "I am fighting for a human life. The life of a hated enemy but nevertheless a life."

**Fact #92: Elaine Fischel—Defense Counsel Staff**

Elaine Fischel graduated from the University of California at Los Angeles (UCLA) in 1940 at the age of 19. Before she became a national college tennis champion, she used to play with her neighborhood friend, Gertrude "Gussie" Moran, who later competed at Wimbledon.

During the war, Fischel worked with the 20th Air Force in a program that was responsible for training B-29 flight engineers. Many of the trainees—her friends—were killed in the Pacific War. Fischel admits that she hated the enemy.

In 1946, Air Force Colonel Leonard Coleman—a pilot and an attorney—knew about Fischel's interest in the law and asked her if she would be interested in working at the war crimes trials in Japan.

Fischel jumped at the chance and ended up on the legal defense team for Admiral Nagano, Admiral Shimada and Lord Keeper of the Privy Seal Kido at the Tokyo War Crimes Trial. Fischel, still an active member of the California bar, was 87 years old when she wrote and published her memoirs, *Defending the Enemy: Justice for the WWII Japanese War Criminals*.

Because of her role at the Tokyo War Crimes Trial, Fischel was able to meet Japan's most powerful military and political leaders and developed life-long relationships with historic persons such as Prince Takamatsu (Emperor Hirohito's younger brother), Ambassador and Admiral Kichisaburo Nomura, Admiral Shigetaro Shimada, Justice B. V. A. Röling, Marquis Koichi Kido (Lord Keeper of the Privy Seal) and John Brannon.

Always in the background of Elaine Fischel's memoirs are the troubling questions: Who defines what a war crime is? What is criminal behavior and what is not during a time when the people of warring nations are trying to annihilate one another?

[Author's Note: In her memoirs, Fischel wrote that George Mizota was a constant behind-the-scenes participant at the Tokyo War Crimes Trial and that "he was the best interpreter in Japan." Because of that description, the author contacted her and was fascinated by her life story. She asked the author to help her make her memoirs available to the Japanese people she had come to love and respect. The translation was recently completed and is expected to be published in Japan in early 2014.

In another small world story, Fischel met Ise Togo on several occasions at the Tokyo War Crimes Trial.]

**Fact #93: Captain Mitsuo Fuchida at the Tokyo War Crimes Trial**

Fuchida, as the leader of the attack on Pearl Harbor, worried from the day of Japan's surrender that the IMTFE would name him a Class-A War Criminal for his role in starting the war with the U.S.

He was, of course, relieved when he found out that he would not be indicted. He was interviewed by the Allied military staff on numerous occasions and was a witness at the Tokyo War Crimes Trial several times.

In his memoirs, Fuchida wrote that he believed that the Tokyo War Crimes Trial was similar to the ancient "feast of the barbarians." The victors simply chopped off the heads of their defeated enemies and placed them around the banquet table where victory was celebrated. In other words, there were no war crimes—except to lose on the battlefield.

In a letter that was discovered decades after the trial, Brannon had written to his brother, Kansas City Chief of Police, that of all the IJN people he met, Mitsuo Fuchida impressed him the most.

[Author's Note: A war slogan chanted by pro-Imperial soldiers during the Meiji Revolution was, "If we win, we are the loyalist army; if we lose, the rebel forces."]

## Fact #94: The Tokyo War Crimes Trial—Prosecution Strategy

The basis for the Allied Powers' legal indictment was two-fold: (1) from the early 1930s, Japan's political and military leaders had conspired to wage war against the people of Far East Asia and the West; and (2) once Japan embarked on a course of aggressive war, it committed many crimes against peace for which its leaders should be held accountable.

The Defense challenged the indictment. Its main argument was that, under the principles of international law then in effect, the concepts of conspiracy and aggressive war were not established as crimes. Furthermore, the Defense argued that there was no precedent or basis in international law for holding individuals responsible for acts of the state.

The Defense argued that the Allied Powers' violations of international law, including the atomic bombings of Japan, should be examined.

Former Foreign Minister Togo argued that Japan had no option but to prosecute the war for self-defense purposes. He maintained "that Japan was being driven either to war or suicide" by the U.S.

**Fact #95: Japanese Prisoners of War in the Soviet Union**

Historians estimate that the Soviet Union imprisoned between 500,000 and 800,000 Japanese troops after the war. The Soviets released them over a period of years, but many died in forced labor camps in Siberia and Mongolia.

When the Japanese prisoners returned to their homeland, their stories about their treatment only strengthened the Japanese people's distrust of the Russians and the Communist system of government.

**Fact #96: The Tokyo War Crimes Trial—The Verdict**

One defendant, Shumei Okawa, had a mental breakdown during the trial, and charges against him were dropped.

Two defendants, Yosuke Matsuoka and Osami Nagano, died of natural causes during the trial.

Seven defendants were sentenced to death by hanging for war crimes, crimes against humanity and crimes against peace:

• General Hideki Tojo
• General Kenji Doihara
• Prime Minister Koki Hirota
• General Seishiro Itagaki
• General Heitaro Kimura
• Lieutenant General Akira Muto
• General Iwane Matsui

The remaining sixteen defendants were sentenced to life imprisonment—among them Brannon's clients, Admiral Shigetaro Shimada, Admiral Takazumi Oka and General Kenryo Sato.

Foreign Minister Shigenori Togo was sentenced to 20 years imprisonment. At the age of 67, while still serving his sentence, he died of heart failure in July, 1950 in a U.S. military hospital.

## Fact #97: The Tokyo War Crimes Trial—Dissenting Voices

Justice Radhabinod Pal of India found all of the defendants not guilty. (India, which effectively became a British colony in 1757, was partitioned in 1947 into the independent nations of India and Pakistan.) Pal wrote that the Tokyo War Crimes Trial was nothing "other than the opportunity for the victors to retaliate." In his opinion, he asserted that the Tribunal incorrectly excluded the long history of Western colonialism and the use of the atom bomb by the United States from the list of crimes.

Justice B. V. A. Röling of the Netherlands stated, "[o]f course, in Japan we were all aware of the bombings and the burnings of Tokyo and Yokohama and other big cities. It was horrible that we went there for the purpose of vindicating the laws of war, and yet saw every day how the Allies had violated them dreadfully."

## Fact #98: John Brannon—After the Tokyo War Crimes Trial

Brannon returned to Kansas City, where he became Missouri's Assistant Attorney General before starting his own law firm. He also was an assistant to U.S. Senator Thomas Hennings and served as Missouri's unofficial Senator during Henning's illness from May through September 1960.

He maintained that Japan and the U.S. were natural allies in the fight against the Soviets and Communism. He died in August, 1987.

## Fact #99: Elaine Fischel—After the Tokyo War Crimes Trial

Fischel returned to the U.S. and applied to law school. When she graduated from the University of Southern California Law School in 1953, she was the only woman in her class. And, of course, she passed the California Bar Exam on her first try.

Recently, Fischel acquired thousands of pages of documents preserved by John Brannon. She donated these documents to the President Harry Truman Library in Independence, Missouri, where they have been cataloged, archived and are available to the public. In November, 2012, Fischel gave a speech at the Truman Library which focused on the importance of the Tokyo War Crimes Trial and on the contribution of John Brannon to international law and justice.

She is an active member of the California Bar.

## Fact #100: Revelations after World War II—Secret Payment to MacArthur by Philippines President Manuel Quezon

In January, 1942, Philippines President Manuel Quezon offered General MacArthur $500,000 as payment for his pre-war service as Field Marshall of the Philippine Army. MacArthur accepted. His U.S. Army staff members also received payments: $75,000 for Lieutenant General Richard Sutherland, his Chief of Staff; $45,000 for General Richard Marshall, and $20,000 for a staff aide, Sidney Huff.

These payments were known to only very few leaders in Manila and Washington, including President Roosevelt and Secretary of War Henry L. Stimson. A memo detailing this matter was discovered in the archives of General Sutherland, and the payments were made public by Professor Carol Petillo of Boston College in her 1981 biography, *Douglas MacArthur: The Philippine Years.*

Petillo wrote: "If greed, resentment, and a need for reassurance explained the acceptance of the money, it is still necessary to examine Quezon's reasons for offering it. Perhaps...the Filipino leader believed that this sum would convince MacArthur to use his influence in Washington to insure relief for the Philippines."

She also noted that "...in the spring of 1942, Manuel Quezon attempted to present a similar 'recompense and reward' to Eisenhower for his service in the Philippines between November 15, 1935 and December 1939..." The offer was reportedly $100,000.

Petillo noted that, "In a Memorandum for Record dated June 20, 1942, the future President of the United States" diplomatically thanked Quezon but turned down his offer. Eisenhower wrote, "that it was inadvisable and even impossible for me to accept a material reward for the services performed. [Emphasis his.]"

**Fact #101: Jardine Matheson—Sailing Full Circle and Continuing Obligations**

The Yasuda "*Zaibatsu*," or conglomerate, was founded by Zenjiro Yasuda in the late 1860s at the end of the Meiji Revolution and became one of the four largest business enterprises in Imperial Japan. It was dismantled at the end of World War II but continued as the Fuyo Business Group.

In the 1990s, Zenjiro Yasuda's great-grandson, Hiroshi Yasuda served as CEO of Jardine Matheson, Japan. In answer to why he was with the Hong Kong-based trading firm and not with one of his family's many companies, Yasuda replied that the "obligation goes back many years and will continue for many years. Jardine Matheson provided rifles from the U.S. and UK that were needed to win the civil war against the Shogunate, as well as the money to finance the rebels' military capability."

Furthermore, former Prime Minister Shigeru Yoshida's father was once a branch manager of Jardine Matheson, Japan. And Yoko Ono Lennon is a great-granddaughter of Zenjiro Yasuda and second cousin of Hiroshi Yasuda.

Jardine Matheson became the first foreign firm registered in Japan a few years after the U.S. Navy forcibly opened Japan to the rest of the world. In 2009, its employees celebrated the trading firm's 150th anniversary in Japan.

# Postscript

Of the eleven judges sitting on the Tribunal of the Tokyo War Crimes Trial, only Justice Radhabinod Pal of India found all of the defendants not guilty. His dissenting opinion was over 700 pages long, and he asserted that the Tribunal incorrectly excluded the long history of Western colonialism in Asia. What the Japanese did, he stated, was no different from what the imperial powers had been doing for centuries.

Justice Pal knew that the forces unleashed by the Pacific War would result in the eventual release of his country from the yoke of British control. What he could not predict was the continuation of the Pacific War.

The signing of the Surrender Treaty in Tokyo Bay on September 2, 1945 ended hostilities between the Allied nations and Japan. Japan's unconditional surrender meant the end of that country's dream of establishing a Greater Asia Co-Prosperity Sphere. It did not end efforts by other countries to achieve a similar objective.

In late 1945, the Dutch tried to re-establish control over the Dutch East Indies. They fought local rebel troops, in what became known as the Indonesian War for Independence, until 1949, when the Netherlands recognized Indonesia as an independent country.

The French initiated their bid to re-assert colonial control over French Indochina in December 1946. What is known as the First Indochina War lasted until August 1954, when the Viet Minh rebels surrounded a garrison of 20,000 French troops at Dien Bien Phu. The French general in charge of the outpost was ordered to surrender rather than face certain annihilation. The new country of Vietnam was granted independence, but the Second Indochina War—better known as the Vietnam War—began shortly after.

In Malaya, local rebels agitated for independence. The British responded by relocating an estimated 500,000 Malayans. By mid-1948, the insurgency had become a serious military matter, and eventually 40,000 British and Commonwealth troops were deployed to Malaya. The prolonged armed conflict was known as the Malayan Emergency because if the British government had called it a war, property and material losses suffered by British owners would not have been covered by their UK-based insurers. A peace treaty was signed in 1960, and the newly independent country of Malaysia was born.

# Bibliography

Abe, Zenji
*The Emperor's Sea Eagle: A Memoir of the Attack on Pearl Harbor and the War in the Pacific*
Arizona Memorial Press 2006

Agawa, Hiroyuki
*The Reluctant Admiral: Yamamoto and the Imperial Navy*
Kodansha International 1979

Alperovitz, Gar
*The Decision to Use the Atomic Bomb: And the Architecture of an American Myth*
Knopf 1995

Arquilla, John
*Insurgents, Raiders, and Bandits: How Masters of Irregular Warfare Have Shaped Our World*
Ivan R. Dee 2011

Boei-cho Boei-Kenshujo, Senshi-shitsu (Japan Self-Defense Ministry, Research Division, War Archives)
*Hawaii Sakusen (Hawaii Operations Plan)*
Asakumo Shinbunsha 1967

Borneman, Walter R.
*The Admirals: Nimitz, Halsey, Leahy, and King—The Five-Star Admirals Who Won the War at Sea*
Little Brown and Company 2012

Clarke, Thurston
*Pearl Harbor Ghosts: The Legacy of December 7, 1941*
Ballantine 2001

Costello, John
*Days of Infamy: MacArthur, Roosevelt, Churchill—The Shocking Truth Revealed*
Pocket Books 1994

Craig, William
*The Fall of Japan*
The Dial Press 1967

Davis, Burke
*The Billy Mitchell Affair*
Random House 1967

D'Este, Carlo
*Warlord: A Life of Winston Churchill at War, 1874-1945*
Harper 2008

Dower, John W.
*Embracing Defeat: Japan in the Wake of World War II*
Norton & Company 1999

Epstein, Jennifer Cody
*The Gods of Heavenly Punishment: A Novel*
W. W. Norton & Company 2013

Evans, David C. and Mark R. Peattie
*Kaigun: Strategy, Tactics and Technology in the Imperial Japanese Navy, 1887-1941*
Naval Institute Press 1997

Evans, David C. (ed)
*The Japanese Navy in World War II: In the Words of Former Japanese Naval Officers, Second Edition*
Naval Institute Press 1986

Fischel, Elaine B.
*Defending the Enemy: Justice for the WWII Japanese War Criminals*
Bascom Hill Books 2010

Fuchida, Mitsuo
*Shinjuwan Kogeki (Attack on Pearl Harbor)*
PHP Bunko 2001

Fuchida, Mitsuo
*Shinjuwan Kogeki Sotaicho no Kaiso (Memoirs of the Leader of the Pearl Harbor Attack)*
Kodansha 2007

Fuchida, Mitsuo and Masatake Okumiya
*Midway: The Battle That Doomed Japan, the Japanese Navy's Story*
Naval Institute Press 2001

Goldstein, Donald M. and Katherine V. Dillon (eds.)
*The Pearl Harbor Papers: Inside the Japanese Plans*
Brassey's 2000

Gordon, Beate Sirota
*The Only Woman in the Room*
Kodansha 2001

Hastings, Max
*Retribution: The Battle for Japan, 1944-45*
Alfred A. Knopf 2008

Hosoya, Chihiro, Nisuki Ando, Yasuaki Onuma, Richard H. Minear
*The Tokyo War Crimes Trial: An International Symposium*
Kodansha International 1986

Hoyt, Edwin P.
*How They Won the War in the Pacific: Nimitz and His Admirals*
Lyons Press 2000

Ienaga, Saburo
*The Pacific War: World War II and the Japanese, 1931-1945*
Random House 1978

Johnson, Galen Irvin
*Defending the Japanese Warlords: The Tokyo War Crimes Trial—A New Perspective*
University of Kansas Unpublished PhD Dissertation 1998

Koven, Steven G. and Frank Götzke
*American Immigration Policy: Confronting the Nation's Challenges*
Springer 2010

Kuhn, Adolph (Pearl Harbor Survivor)
*An American Journey (1921-Present)*
Self-Published 2009

Layton, Edwin T., Roger Pineau and John Costello
*And I Was There: Pearl Harbor and Midway Breaking the Secrets*
William Morris & Co. 1995

Leary, William M. (ed.)
*MacArthur and the American Century: A Reader*
"An Exchange of Opinion—Paul P. Rogers, Virginia Polytechnic Institute and State University, and Carol M. Petillo"
University of Nebraska Press 2001

Miller, Edward S.
*Bankrupting the Enemy: The U.S. Financial Siege of Japan before Pearl Harbor*
Naval Institute Press 2007

Miller, Edward S.
*War Plan Orange: The U.S. Strategy to Defeat Japan, 1897-1945*
Naval Institute Press 1991

Peattie, Mark R.
*Sunburst: The Rise of Japanese Naval Air Power, 1909-1941*
Naval Institute Press 2001

Petillo, Carol Morris
*Douglas MacArthur: The Philippine Years*
University of Indiana 1981

Potter, E. B.
*Nimitz*
Naval Institute Press 1976

Prange, Gordon W. with Donald M. Goldstein and Katherine V. Dillon
*At Dawn We Slept: The Untold Story of Pearl Harbor*
Penguin Books 1991

Prange, Gordon W. with Donald M. Goldstein and Katherine V. Dillon
*Dec. 7 1941: The Day the Japanese Attacked Pearl Harbor*
McGraw-Hill 1988

Prange, Gordon W. with Donald M. Goldstein and Katherine V. Dillon
*Miracle at Midway*
MJF Books 1982

Prange, Gordon W. with Donald M. Goldstein and Katherine V. Dillon
*Pearl Harbor: The Verdict of History*
Penguin Books 1991

Prange, Gordon W. with Donald M. Goldstein and Katherine V. Dillon
*Target Tokyo: The Story of the Sorge Spy Ring*
McGraw-Hill 1984

Reel, A. Frank
*The Case of General Yamashita*
University of Chicago Press 1949

Ryan, Allan A.
*Yamashita's Ghost: War Crimes, MacArthur's Justice, and Command Accountability*
University Press of Kansas 2012

Shinsato, Douglas T. and Tadanori Urabe (Translators)
*For That One Day: The Memoirs of Mitsuo Fuchida, Commander of the Attack on Pearl Harbor*
eXperience, inc. 2011

Sledge, E. B.
*With the Old Breed: At Peleliu and Okinawa*
Presidio Press 2007

Togo, Shigehiko
*Sofu Togo Shigenori no Shogai (The Biography of Shigenori Togo, My Grandfather)*
Bungei Shunju 1993

Togo, Shigenori
*The Cause of Japan (by the Foreign Minister of Japan at the Time of Pearl Harbor and Again at the End of the Pacific War)*
Simon and Schuster 1956

Truman, Harry S.
*Off the Record: The Private Papers of Harry S. Truman (Edited by Robert H. Ferrell)*
Harper & Row 1980

Unger, Frederic William
*Russia and Japan: And a Complete History of the War in the Far East*
W. E. Scull 1904

Wilmott, H. P.
*Empires in the Balance: Japanese and Allied Pacific Strategies to April 1942*
Naval Institute Press 1982

Wilmottt, H. P. with Tohmatsu Haruo and W. Spencer Johnson
*Pearl Harbor*
Cassell & Co 2001

Yergin, Daniel
*The Prize: The Epic Quest for Oil, Money and Power*
Simon & Schuster 1991

Made in the USA
Charleston, SC
04 December 2015